A POPULAR TRACT

ON

CHURCH MUSIC,

WITH REMARKS

ON

ITS MORAL AND POLITICAL IMPORTANCE,

AND A PRACTICAL

Scheme for its Reformation.

BY

ROBERT DRUITT, ESQ.

"I much distrust the symmetry of their heads who declaim against Church Music. There is something in it of Divinity more than the ear discovers."

SIR T. BROWNE'S RELIGIO MEDICI.

LONDON:

FRANCIS & JOHN RIVINGTON,

ST. PAUL'S CHURCH YARD, AND WATERLOO PLACE.

MDCCCXLV.

PREFACE.

THE writer begs respectfully to call the attention of the clergy and laity to the present neglected state of Church Music.

Considering that the Church of England possesses a rich store of music, derived, in great measure, from the times of primitive Christianity, which harmonizes admirably, both in tone and style and feeling, with the habits of cheerful intellectual piety which her services inculcate, it certainly is to be lamented, that this should be suffered to fall into oblivion, and to be replaced by an inferior style of psalmody, which has always been the very characteristic of dissent.

But whether or not the writer has been success-ful in pointing out the principles on which our congregational service should be reformed, or in devising a scheme for carrying those principles into execution, he feels that the attempt will require no apology in the eyes of any one who wishes the Church to be loved as well as respected, or who desires to train the affections and imaginations, as well as the mere intellect of our rising generation.

39 A, Curzon-street, May-fair, London,
May 17th, 1845.

CONTENTS.

	PAGE
Miserable state of Church Music in most parishes	7
Right and wrong principles of reformation	8
Nature of Common Prayer	9
Benefits of carrying out the spirit of our Liturgy	10
Theory of chanting	15
Popular prejudices	18
Metrical versions of the Psalms	24
Prose versions	26
Theory of music	31
Characteristics of Church Music	33
Introduction of secular compositions into church	38
Gregorian tones	40
Modern hymn-tunes	42
Hymns ancient and modern	43
Music at the celebration of the Lord's Supper	45
Scheme for parochial Church Music associations	46
Benefits of clerical and episcopal superintendence	51
Abuses of the organ	52
Musical education for the people	54
Political and social benefits	56
State of the Church	57
Æsthetics of religion	59
Causes of dissent	60
Conclusion	61

A

POPULAR TRACT,

&c.

THE musical part of divine service in most parish churches is well known to be most wretched; but yet both the taste for music, and the means of learning it, have been widely extended of late years; insomuch that there are few families, above the very poorest orders, some member of which cannot play or sing. Vast sums are every year expended on the theatre and concert-room. The people who frequent the opera, would look on it as a piece of most disgraceful niggardliness, if the best *artistes* were not engaged at their own prices. But, strange to say, they who frequent churches seem to consider neither care, nor skill, nor expense, necessary; but are content with the performance of one or two indifferent psalm-tunes by charity children, who cannot pronounce their own language with decency.

And not only the music, but that part of the service also which is assigned to the congregation, is treated with the utmost neglect. People sit silently in their pews, and leave the responses to be said by the clerk and children; hence a coldness and languor, a want of fervency and earnestness, about the whole service.

It is true that various attempts have been made to remedy these evils, but without much success; and the object of the writer is to show that the want of success may have depended on the wrong direction in which those efforts were made, and to point out something like a principle by which future attempts may perhaps procure greater success.

The wrong direction in which these efforts were made, we believe to be this: psalms or hymns have been introduced into the intervals of the service; they may have been sung with more or less skill, and have been joined in by a greater or less number of the congregration;—but yet they have been made to appear as something quite distinct from the service itself; and those parts of the service which ought to be sung or said aloud by the people, are still barely whispered, or left to the clerk and children.

On the other hand, the right principle on which a reformation should be based, should be to make the Liturgy itself the source of interest and attraction; to devote all our musical resources to its devout and solemn celebration; and not, as at present, to let the Liturgy and exultant Psalms of David be tamely repeated, and the responses quietly whispered, the congregation all the time falling into a state of weariness and ennui, from which they are glad to be roused by a hymn, or a loud voluntary on the organ.

In fact, instead of employing hymns and voluntaries in the intervals of the service, as a relief to its monotony and sameness, we ought so to perform the service, as to make itself the source of delight, and bring into play that admirable variety and alternation of prayer, praise, and thanksgiving, which it contains. How inconsistent it seems to refuse the aid of music to the noble hymns in which the daily Liturgy abounds, and expend it all on supplementary hymns, which are not wanted, which are inferior in every respect, and which seriously add to what men complain of—the length of the service.

Now in order to develope the principle for which we contend, we must first direct attention to one point respecting the nature of our service, which is hardly enough considered. We must then observe, that the service of the Church is not a *private*, but a *public* service; not *individual* prayer, but *common* prayer; not relating so much to private persons or families, as to the whole Christian community; not to affairs of personal or domestic happiness, not so much to those things which ought to be prayed for, by every one in private, or by families, as to what all hold in common,—the acknowledgment of sin, the supplication of forgiveness, prayers for the welfare of the whole Catholic Church, confessions of the true faith, praise for the means of grace and for the hope of glory. So comprehensive, indeed, is it, that every man may find in it that which applies to his own individual case; but yet, whilst joining in the Liturgy, he is not praying merely for himself, or by himself, as if he were in his own closet or family; on the contrary, he is joining in a public common act of the congregation of which he is a member.

Not that we should abstain from urging our own private supplications when assembled as members of a congregation; but we should not do so to the neglect of the more important duty of public worship. "This holy and religious duty of service towards God," says Richard Hooker, "concerneth us one way in that we are men, and another way in that we are joined as parts to that visible mystical body, which is his church. As men, we are at our own choice, both for time, and place, and form, according to the exigence of our occasions in private; but the service which we do as members of a public body, is public, and for that cause must needs be accounted so much worthier than the other, as a whole society of such condition exceedeth the worth of any one[2]."

When, then, men are by themselves, they may use any form they please; whether they prefer open speech, or silent meditation: but in the public congregation, they have a public duty; so that they might say to an infidel, or an heathen, if present, This is our faith; these are our prayers; these are the principles in which we live, and in which we hope to die.

Now it not unfrequently happens that well-meaning persons speak of being *disturbed in their devotions* by some one who repeats the responses aloud in a neighbouring pew; a proof how little the real nature of the Liturgy is understood, when one who joins in it according to its real spirit, is considered a cause of interruption and disturbance,—as if it were merely mental prayer or meditation that we had met to join in, like Quakers or Dissenters, who have no common prayer.

But it surely cannot require much argument to show the benefits that might reasonably be expected from a fuller concurrence with the spirit of the Liturgy. In the first place, an increase of devotional feeling amongst the people. At present there is a strange feeling of shame which prevents

<hr />

[2] Ecclesiastical Polity, book v. sect. 24.

men from alluding to their religion as a principle of their lives; (as a matter of politics or doctrinal dispute, unhappily it is but too frequently brought forward;) or of being seen more deeply engaged in devotion than their neighbours. "Which of us," says a witty writer, "dare sing psalms aloud in church?" How many an opportunity of doing good and checking sin is lost, through shame of appearing unusually godly:—the same shame which seals our lips in church lest our neighbours should laugh at us.

Then consider the effect produced on a stranger, or an habitual sinner, or on one who has long been without the opportunity of joining in public worship, or still more on a heathen. What is there to rouse the attention, or to warm the heart, in the dull listless service of our parish churches? Could a heathen believe us in earnest when we commit the offering up our solemn praise to God to a bellowing organ and screaming children? Would he be likely, as St. Paul says, when urging a decent and impressive mode of celebrating divine service, to "fall down on his face, and worship God, and report that God is in us of a truth?"

Next, let us allude to the increased feeling of Christian brotherhood which would pervade all classes, if they were made to feel that they are not to go to God's house to be installed in a luxurious cushioned pew, close-curtained from the vulgar gaze, and their refined devotions undisturbed by the ejaculations of their poorer neighbours; but rather to cast off all worldly consequence at the threshold, and to consider the intercessions of the poor for their deliverance from the perils of wealth, as a greater benefit than they can repay by the mere superfluities of their worldly goods.

Again, might it not be expected to diminish the feeling of distance and want of sympathy, which, especially in large towns, there is between the minister and a great portion of his flock? How many ever dream of consulting their clergyman on their own spiritual state, unless they happen to be on their death-bed! And when they meet in church, what is the common idea? That he is to lead and direct their devotions, to pray for them and with them? No: but that the *reader* (as he is called) is to read to them, and much they dwell on the sonorousness of his voice[1].

---

[1] The judicious Hooker treats so admirably on this point, that I cannot refrain from a quotation, long though it be. And I may add, that if this most heavenly-minded man's works were more read and acted upon, there would have been no occasion for this poor pamphlet :

"If the prophet David did think that the very meeting of men together, and their accompanying one another to the house of God, should make the band of their love indissoluble, and tie them in a league of insoluble unity; how much more may we judge it reasonable to hope that the like results may grow in each of the people towards other—in them all

Now if, as we hope, we have shown the real
nature of our Common Prayer, and some of the

towards their pastor, and in their pastor towards every of
them, between whom there daily and interchangeably pass, in
the hearing of God Himself and in presence of his holy angels,
so many heavenly acclamations, exultations, provocations, peti-
tions, songs of comfort, psalms of praise and thanksgiving? In
all which particulars, as when the pastor maketh their suits, and
they, with one voice, testify a general assent thereunto * ; or
when he joyfully beginneth, and they with like alacrity follow,
dividing between them the sentences wherewith they strive
which shall most show his own and stir up others' zeal to the
glory of that God whose name they magnify † ; or when he
proposeth unto God their necessities, and they their own requests for relief in every of them ‡ ; or when he lifteth up his
voice like a trumpet, to proclaim unto them the laws of God,
they adjoining (though not as Israel did, by way of generality and
cheerful promise, " All that the Lord hath commanded, we will
do ;" yet that which God doth no less approve, that which
savoureth more of meekness, that which testifieth rather a
feeling knowledge of our common infirmity), unto the several
branches thereof, several lowly and humble requests for grace
at the merciful hands of God, to perform the thing that is commanded § ; or when they wish reciprocally each other's ghostly
happiness || ; or when he by exhortation raiseth them up, and
they by protestation of their readiness declare he speaketh not in

---

* Amen.
† In the suffrages.
‡ In the litany.
§ Commandments.
|| " The Lord be with you, And with thy spirit."

benefits which might be expected, were the congregation to join audibly in the service according to its original intent, we shall be asked how they can be induced to do so.

Now it will be found undoubtedly true, that when any body of people are assembled together, actuated by the same feeling, and that an earnest one; all saying the same thing at the same time, and for the same purpose, they invariably speak together in the same tone—that is to say, they make use of a musical intonation and rhythm. In such a case, music is the very rhetoric of nature. It is the means by which we give emphasis, and ensure unanimity;—by which the prevailing passion is expressed, enforced, and propagated. The cheers of a mob, the cries of sailors whilst weighing anchor, and the shouts of children, are familiar but sufficient illustrations.

So long as the human ear possesses its faculties, it will be impossible to produce the general simultaneous response in plain unmusical tones. The voice, as employed in ordinary speech, varies half a tone, or more, at irregular intervals; more if a person speaks with much animation and emphasis;

vain * ; those interlocutory forms of speech,—what are they else but most effectual, partly provocations, and partly inflammations of all piety ?" *Sect.* 39.

---

* " Lift up your hearts !—We lift them up unto the Lord."

and more generally in the speech of foreigners, and of the Scotch and Irish, than in that of the English. Hence it follows, that when a number of people are repeating the same thing at the same time, without attention to the tone in which they speak, each voice has its own degree and quantity of variation in tone, and the effect of the whole is most discordant to the ear.

And so it happens in church ; whilst reciting the Creed or Psalms, the ear is offended with the variety of discords produced by the voices of neighbouring people ; and, however devout or attentive the congregation may be, they drop off insensibly one by one and keep silence, without knowing the reason : those first who have the acutest ears. The only persons who do keep up their recitation to the end, are the clerk and children ; and the latter will always be found, however unconsciously, to speak in a uniform tone. In fact, when a common sentiment is expressed by a number of persons in musical intonation and rhythm, it resembles the measured tread of a well-disciplined regiment ; its very order is expressive of earnestness, solemnity, and force. But the same thing murmured prosaically resembles rather the disorderly walk of a rabble, confused, jostling each other, with stragglers dropping off on all sides.

Thus then we would urge, that for the due celebration of the Liturgy, it is necessary to use some kind of musical tone, such as is customary in our Cathedrals; the minister saying his part in a certain tone, and the people responding in the same, with some degree of modulation and harmony. But we are fully aware of the host of objections which many well-meaning people would raise against such an idea; and we wish to devote a little space to the consideration of these objections. For, strange to say, so uninformed are the mass of the community as to the history and constitution of their own church, that they are apt to exclaim against the most ancient and laudable custom as a superstitious innovation, if it do not happen to accord with what themselves have been used to.

Now many people object to the musical intonation of the responses,—those portions of the Liturgy in which, to use Hooker's words, their pastor "joyfully beginneth, and they with like alacrity follow, dividing between them the sentences, wherewith they strive which shall most show his own and stir up others' zeal to the glory of that God whose name they magnify." A common expression is, that people are not used to it, and that it disturbs their devotions. To this we may reply, that if useful, mere liking or disliking ought not to be taken into account, and that it will never disturb the devotions of those who heartily join in it. But the gravest objection which we hear is, that it is irreverent and unnatural to sing our prayers, and that, as

B

we should not use a singing tone whilst presenting
a petition to our earthly sovereign, so neither ought
we to do so when offering our prayers to the King
of kings.

But in defence of the use of a musical tone (or
chant) for the Liturgy, it will suffice to state the fact,
that it has been customary to use it in every branch
of the Christian church from the remotest antiquity,
and in the Jewish church long before ; and the principle upon which it was doubtless adopted, and for
which it ought to be continued is, that in addressing
the Almighty in a public set form of service, it is
not right to use the ordinary tone of trivial conver-
sation, but one that is more solemn, requiring more
care for its enunciation, more calculated to arouse
the attention, and to remind the listener that they
are not the things of this world that he now has to
think of.

And such is the effect which the solemn old
tones of our Cathedral responses produce, on every
one who enters the church to pray and not to gaze
about, and whose mind is not previously filled with
prejudices against a thing of which he never has
taken the trouble to ascertain the origin, or nature,
or right use. Certainly one who has been accustomed to hear in a Cathedral the praise of God
uttered in tones like these:

Priest.

O Lord,   open   Thou   our   lips:

People.

And   our mouth shall shew forth Thy   praise.

Priest.

O   God, make   speed   to   save   us:

People.

O Lord, make   haste   to   help   us.

and then in some London parish church hears the same spoken in a cold, prosaic tone by the priest, whilst the wretched children to whom the inhabitants of the richest city of the world commit the duty of making the response, answer in mouth-contracting cockneyisms,

"Ô Lôd ma' kaste t'elp's:"

such an one will not think that the irreverence lies on the side of the Cathedral service.

Besides, the suffrages which are said responsively by priest and people are all portions of some Psalm, and we would ask what possible harm there can be in singing them as they occur in the Liturgy, if there be no harm in singing them when converted into metre. The responses we have just quoted are taken from the 51st and 70th Psalms; the following is also taken from the 51st Psalm: and we would ask how any rational person, who would not object to sing it to a common psalm-tune when thus disguised and dilated in the metrical version of Brady and Tate—

"Create in me an heart that's clean, an upright mind renew,
    Withdraw not Thou thy help, nor cast me from thy sight,
    Nor let thy Holy Spirit take its everlasting flight:"

could yet demur at joining in the following tones, breathing, as they do, the spirit of the most earnest and heartfelt supplication:

Minister.

O God, make clean our hearts with---in us:

People.

And take not   Thy   Ho-----ly   Spi---rit   from   us.

To those who complain that the chanting prayers
not what men would *naturally* do if in earnest,
ꞓ would put the question, which of the above
odes of addressing the throne of heaven is the
ore simple and natural?   Supposing both equally
ꞓed in the memory, which is more congenial to
.e mind of one who wished to pray in earnest?
It would occupy too much space were we enter
to a consideration of the terms, *natural, state of
iture,* &c., terms which are so often used in argu-
ent by illogical people, who say, for instance, that
if we were living in a *state of nature*, we should
· should not do so and so."   Now, if by state of
iture is meant, that man, originally

" ——— wild in woods a noble savage ran,"

iat he was only a better kind of ape; that laws, arts,
id civilization, have been the developments of his
iaided mind, which have raised him gradually
om this state of nature; and that all the comforts,

ornaments, and decencies, of polished society, are all deviations from this supposed state; we reply, that this is a mere atheistical fiction, having no foundation in history or experience. But the Christian, whilst admitting and lamenting that man's nature is sadly depraved by the sin of our first father, so that we can do no good thing of ourselves, yet believes that man was created in the image of God; endowed with the most noble faculties of imagination and intellect, to cultivate which is one of his highest duties and privileges, and the source of many of his purest pleasures. Whatever, therefore, the cultivated intellect of the civilised man does universally like, that we may assert it is natural for him to like; and hence we can argue, from the universal consent of all nations, that when (as in addressing the Deity) grand and awful sentiments are clothed in sublime language, the tone in which they are recited should be in a corresponding degree, elevated, sonorous, and modulated by art.

So far from being unnatural, we assert that it is in the highest degree natural, when under any strong emotion, to break forth into singing. True, the cold, artificial tone of fashionable English society, self-wrapped, apathetic, which repudiates all show of feeling, or every thing *that is likely to cause a scene*, which teaches that a gentleman should never seem moved,—that is against it; and some persons, doubtless, would find themselves far less at their ease, if mingled with a crowd of worshippers lifting up their voices in hearty devotion, than lolling in their pew, and listening to the parish clerk ;—all around them as quiet and formal as they could wish ; nothing to make them feel *uncomfortable*. Besides, our service in church is not a mere extempore effusion, dictated by the spur of the moment; but is, as it ought to be, ordered and arranged beforehand, so that every thing may be said and done in the manner most reverential and solemn.

We will not pursue this line of argument further; for we feel confident that the more the objections which are brought against the chanting of the Liturgy are analyzed and reasoned upon, the more vague and unsubstantial do they become. We would only request men to study and inquire, and we are sure that they will be convinced.

But if it be expedient that the responses should be chanted, in order that the service may be properly performed by the congregation, all the preceding arguments apply with double force to the Psalms of the day, the Te Deum, and the other canonical hymns. There can be no doubt that they were always intended to be sung : but what a strange inconsistency is evident in most churches ? we go out of our way to introduce hymns, or portions of Psalms in metre, into the intervals of the

Liturgy, whilst those very Psalms which are appointed as our daily portion of praise, and which, if
properly performed, would render the others unne-
cessary, are not sung at all.   Day by day, the absurdity, we might almost call it mockery, is committed,
of minister and congregation repeating the earnest
invitation, " O come let us sing unto the Lord," and
yet not singing ;—of calling on the heavens, the
earth, and the sea, to rejoice before the Lord ; of
asking for every instrument of music, lutes, harps,
and psalteries ; and of exhorting each other to
" sing lustily with a good courage ;"—and the result
of this, is our lazy muttering ; even if the lips of
half the congregation are not entirely quiescent.

If any argument were wanted to show the im-
propriety of tamely reading the regular Psalms that
are appointed to be sung, and of introducing portions of others in metre, it might readily be drawn
from the extreme inferiority of the metrical version
to the prose translation, whether that contained in
the Bible or in the Prayer Book.   It is very certain that the Hebrew poetry cannot be rendered
into English verse without robbing it of its very
peculiar beauties ;—its terseness, the force of its
expressions, the peculiar antithetic construction of
the sentences, most of the excellencies, in fact, on
which its power of impressing the heart and ad-
hering to the memory depend.   Little or none of
those solemn, thrilling feelings of respect and awe,

which are produced by reading a sublime passage of the Psalms or Prophets in the common version, would be felt if the same passage were turned into metre and rhyme. Who that reads a Psalm for devotion or instruction, ever reads it in Brady and Tate? In order to render the words metrical, and to make the lines correspond with the original, expressions require to be lengthened out and diluted, till they have lost their terseness and vigour; others to be added, which have no authority from the original, but merely help to fill up the line. The Psalms in the Hebrew are divided into verses, not according to the number of syllables, but according to the sentiment;—each line generally containing some distinct proposition. There are few epithets or redundancies, few long sentences, in which any grammatical period is continued through several verses;—on the contrary, each line is a distinct clause. But the English metre is a Procrustean contrivance, in which every clause of the original must be lengthened out into sixteen or twenty syllables.

> "Hear my voice, O God, in my prayer,
> Preserve my life from fear of the enemy;
> Hide me from the gathering together of the froward,
> From the insurrection of wicked doers."—PSALM lxiv.

"Lord, hear the voice of my complaint, *to my request give ear*,
Preserve my life from *cruel* foes, *and free my soul from* fear.
O hide me *with thy tenderest care*, in some secure retreat,
From sinners that against me rise, and *all their plots defeat*."

It has often been wondered that no good poet has ever translated the Psalms into metre. But the fact is, no good poet would now attempt it; it would be entirely against the genius of the Hebrew language;—a paraphrase or imitation may be made, and a few clever ones do exist (especially those in which the Psalms are christianized and made to speak in the language of the Gospel dispensation); but a metrical translation is impossible[2].

Let any one compare a metrical version, with a literal prose translation from the Hebrew, and then see how immeasurably superior the latter is in all the essentials of good poetry. Let us take for instance the 137th Psalm. The poet describes the Hebrew captives sitting by the rivers of Babylon, and weeping for their lost father-land.

> " By the waters of Babylon, there sat we down,
>   Yea, we wept when we remembered Sion;
>   Our harps we hanged upon the willows that are in the
>   midst thereof."

[2] " A poem," says Bishop Lowth, " translated literally from the Hebrew into the prose of any other language, whilst the same forms of the sentences remain, will still retain, even as far as relates to versification, much of its native dignity, and a faint appearance of versification. This is evident in our common version of the Scriptures." But " a Hebrew poem, if translated into Greek or Latin [we may add English] verse, and having the conformation of the sentences accommodated to the idiom of a foreign language, will appear confused and mutilated; will scarcely retain a trace of its genuine elegance and peculiar beauty." On Hebrew Poetry, Lecture 3.

This is a picture sketched by a master's hand : it embodies all that is simple, pathetic, and dignified, and excludes all that is mean, irrelevant, and trivial.

But let us see how our English versifiers have copied the picture.

First, Sternhold and Hopkins :—

" When we did sit in Babylon, the rivers round about,
  Then in remembrance of Sion, the tears *for grief* burst out ;
  We hanged our harps *and instruments* the willow trees upon,
  For in that place men for their use had planted many one."

Who wants to know why the willow-trees were there ? Moreover, is it true that they were planted by men, and not rather wild shrubs growing on the river bank ? But what has this mean and trivial interpolation to do with the sense of the Psalm ?

Next, Brady and Tate, the more polished but inanimate of our authorized versifiers :—

" When we *our wearied limbs to rest,* sat down by *proud
      Euphrates'* stream,
  We wept *with doleful thoughts opprest,* and Zion was our
      mournful theme ;
  Our harps, *that, when with joy we sung, were wont their tune-
      ful parts to bear,*
  With silent strings neglected hung, on willow-trees that
      withered there."

How completely the grace and beauty of the

original is buried under this load of verbiage; how completely these dull

"—— expletives their feeble aid do join,"

to swamp all that curt, accurate, and sententious style, which is the very beauty and characteristic of the Hebrew poetry. The Psalmist shows us his countrymen sitting on the ground—the very attitude brings to our mind their dejection and grief; their harps hanging on the willows tell us better than ten thousand words, that they were not in a mood to sing the songs of Zion. But our versifiers, with inherent littleness of mind, take care to leave nothing to our imagination. Their captives sit—because *their limbs are weary!* — they sit too by the river *Euphrates!*—they weep, because *their thoughts are doleful!*—and the cause of their tears, is a *mournful* one! Their harps, we learn, were used as accompaniments to the voice when they sung;—but now that they are not used, they are *neglected;*—and whilst they are not played, they are *silent!*

Let us compare, too, with the original, that somewhat free paraphrase of this Psalm, which Lord Byron has introduced into his Hebrew Melodies; not to criticize it as a mere version of the Psalm, which it was never intended for, but to make an estimate of its relative merits as a poem.

" We sat down and wept by the waters
     Of Babel, and thought of ————

of what? of Zion, says the Psalmist, and our mind supplies the rest; but, according to Lord Byron, they thought of

" ———— —— ———— ———— the day
   When our foe *in the hue of his slaughters* (*!*)
     Made Salem's high places his prey,
   And ye, oh her desolate daughters,
     Were scatter'd all weeping away."

Which is the better poet, the simple Hebrew or the English lord? but Lord Byron's stanzas are not like the tumid verbosities of Brady and Tate[3].

If any one calls this hyper-criticism, and is content with a metrical version of the Psalms on the plea that it is *good enough*, we can only answer that an indifferent thing can surely not be good enough for the service of God when a better can be had; and that certainly it is the height of foolishness to neglect a good thing which we have already, and expend infinite pains in procuring another which

[3] That rule which Sir Joshua Reynolds laid down respecting painting, holds good also in poetry; " the detail of particulars which does not assist the expression of the main characteristic, is worse than useless: it is mischievous, as it dissipates the attention."

can never be good. We would only ask any
person to take any passage in the Psalms that he
happens to be familiar with; whether from its own
beauty, or from its congeniality to his own peculiar
circumstances, and then search it out in any metrical version, and see whether it seem the same.

It is one remarkable property of the sacred poetry,
that there is none which is so profitable to be committed to memory, and none which is so easy. This
arises from the short sententious emphatic clauses
into which it is moulded, which most generally are
arranged so that all the short sentences or lines
have a certain parallelism: that is, similarity in
structure, sentiment, and diction, to each other.
Hence their connection is easily traced even by children; they are soon learned and long retained; in
fact, "the words of the wise" are, like goads, sharp
and impressive; and, "like nails," they penetrate
deeply and get a fast hold. And if there was any
one benefit which we might confidently predict, if
the Psalms were properly chanted by the congregation, it is storing the memory of the young with
such admirable wisdom—wisdom even for the con-
duct of this life—as the Psalms contain. Whilst
learning to chant them, they are almost unconsciously committed to memory. And who that
know what little accidents (as we call them) may
sway the mind for good or for evil, will deny
that some short text, showing that "the righteous

shall never be forsaken," that " the wicked shall be consumed, and that speedily, whilst hope remaineth for the righteous "—forgotten though it may have been for years, might yet act as a balm to a wounded spirit, and prevent the wretchedness of desperation, or just turn the scale when wavering between vice and virtue[3]?

From the comparison of the prose translation with the metrical versions of the Psalms, we proceed naturally to consider the music by which they are accompanied.

Into the general nature of music, and of its power of producing various impressions on our minds, it is not our place now to enter. Yet we may observe, that it seems to consist originally in an imitation of those sounds which we spontaneously make when under the influence of any kind of emotion ;—and as the expression of emotion

---

[3] " What is there necessary for men to know, that the Psalms are not able to teach ? They are to beginners an easy and familiar introduction, a mighty augmentation of all virtue and knowledge in such as entered before, a strong confirmation to the most perfect amongst others. Heroical magnanimity, exquisite justice, grave moderation, exact wisdom, repentance unfeigned, unwearied patience, the mysteries of God, the sufferings of Christ, the terrors of wrath, the comforts of grace, the works of Providence over this world, and the promised joys of that which is to come, all good necessary to be either known, or done, or had, this one celestial fountain yieldeth."—Hooker, op. cit. b. iv. sect. 37.

suffices to excite it, so musical sounds have the power
of exciting that particular emotion whose natural
mode of expression they imitate.   Under the influence of grief and despondency the tones of voice
are low and plaintive, and their utterance slow and
monotonous ;—in joy and exultation they are loud
and animated, and their utterance rapid and emphatic.   And as we can tell by the tones of a
person's voice, whether he is sorrowing or joyful,
even though we may not understand one word of
what he actually says ;—so by music alone we can
be impressed with a particular sentiment of cheerfulness or melancholy, although it may not let us
understand the particular cause or subject of the
sentiment.

Then, whilst certain great classes of musical sounds
are capable of representing certain broad and well-
marked kinds of emotion,—joy or grief for example,—various modifications (*orders* we might techni-
cally say) of the same class of sounds are capable—
partly perhaps through their inherent nature and
propriety, partly through our constant associations—
of raising in our minds the ideas of corresponding
modifications of the sentiment.   Thus there is a
difference between the military march and the
dance tune, the comic song and the drinking song;
though all alike are cheerful, rapid, and animating;
and there is a difference between the funeral
march, the religious hymn, and the plaintive love

song, though all alike slow and pathetic; and we are able to distinguish the various minor kinds of sentiment intended to be conveyed, and also to discern a kind of congruity in the music to the sentiment with which it is associated.

Then taking man as a civilized being, capable of being swayed by many kinds and degrees of emotion, there can be little doubt but that each of these can be expressed, more or less accurately, in music; and it becomes our task to inquire what kind of music is best adapted for the service of the Church.

And here we may observe, that a distinction should always be drawn between sacred music as a whole, and that variety of it which should be introduced into churches; because there are many compositions which, although good in themselves, and appropriate vehicles for religious sentiment, and well suited for the chamber or the oratorio, are yet not sufficiently reverential and solemn in their style for the worship of Almighty God, in that house where we more immediately seek his presence.

For Christians ought to feel love to their Lord, and to rejoice in his holy name; they ought also as sinners to feel sorrow and shame for their transgressions, and supplicate forgiveness with all humility and lowliness: yet neither their joy nor their sorrow can be expressed, with propriety, in quite the same tones as if they related to things of this

C

world. There should be a quality about them showing our consciousness of the infinite distance between us and our Maker, and of the overwhelming consequence of the service we offer before Him.

Difficult as it is to express one's ideas on such an intangible subject, yet we will endeavour to mention a few particulars respecting church music, both of what it ought to be, and of what it ought not to be ; considering it as the vehicle and expression of our sentiments when engaged in the most awful of our duties.

In the first place, then, it ought, like everything else offered to Almighty God, to be as good as possible; to be selected from the works of those composers who have exhibited intellect as well as piety in their musical productions. And we cannot possibly have a better test of what is excellent than the well known canon of Longinus. It is not that which somewhat pleases at first, but soon by repetition becomes flat and wearisome : but on the contrary, that which the more it is contemplated the grander does it appear ; till at length it gains entire possession of the mind, fixing itself inseparably as part of its being ; "filling it with transport and an inward pride; the soul delighting in it as though it were its own invention."

Such are the feelings with which every true lover of music rejoices in the sterling productions of our great church composers.   Heard for the first time, the mind can hardly, perhaps, comprehend them in the full extent and depth of their beauty and grandeur.   They appear, perhaps, intricate and confused, and the mind feels painfully its unsuccessful effort to grasp their noble ideas.   But repeated again and again, light gradually breaks in upon the soul ; the obscure and confused shows only a more wonderful order ; intertwining harmonies are found " in linked sweetness long drawn out ;" till at length they fix themselves indelibly in the memory, where we trust they will remain long after our mortal clay shall have been turned into kindred dust.

Take, on the other hand, a modern *popular* psalm-tune—how soon it becomes inexpressibly wearisome and monotonous ; what an absence of all intellect does it generally exhibit—if plaintive, how dismal ; if cheerful, how vulgarly boisterous.

A second point we would urge is, that church music, in its phrases and modes of expression—in what may be called its *common-places*, should have little or no affinity with the secular or theatrical music of the day.   It should be felt that there is as much difference between the style of church and of profane music, as between the language of the Liturgy and the flippant dialogue of a comedy [4].

[4] The reverse is well exemplified by Rossini's *Stabat Mater*, in which strains that begin in tolerable purity, degenerate suddenly into the most theatrical roulades.

In the next place, we would contend that old music, as a general rule, is better than new. Not, as some bigoted people think, that nothing is good which is *not* old; for in all ages the proportion between good and bad is nearly alike. But the flimsy and trivial soon vanish from the face of the earth, whilst that only which is really good is handed down to posterity. So that its having survived to be old, is not the cause, but the effect, of the estimation in which it is held.

Again, old music will have the advantage of being at least free from any resemblance to the conventional prettinesses of the day. As in language, so in music, every age has its set of mannerisms, which are heard often enough in the secular music of the day, but which ought never to find their way into the church. There always will be some popular composers for the theatre, and they will be closely followed by the band of flimsy song-writers about love and beauty, whose trash is spawned in abundance daily, and perishes before it sees the next year's sun. Their common phrases, will, as it were, be the *musical cant* of the day. If we hear these in church, we feel that there is a something less reverent than there should be. But although we cannot suppose the old masters to have been entirely free from the conventionalities of their day, yet the contemporary fashions and frivolities, having vanished from the earth, they now can bring to our recollection none of the pomps and vanities of the outer world. In the music of Tallis or Tye may be found some passages which remind one of an ancient madrigal of their day; but this, even if known, would bring with it no irreverent associations [5].

Besides this, there is something terse, quaint, and to the purpose in old music, which, like the contemporary language, is well contrasted with the more familiar and diffuse style of the present day [6]. Take, for instance, the Doxology before the reading of the Holy Gospel. Tallis gives it as one exulting acclamation—

Glo - ry be to Thee, O Lord.

Not so a modern composer: he spins it out:—

[5] In a Te Deum of Tallis, the passage "We believe that Thou shalt come to be our Judge," reminds us forcibly of the madrigal "Down in a Flow'ry Vale."

[6] Compare also the response "O Lord, make haste to help us," at page 19, with anything in modern style, and observe its dignified simplicity.

Glo - ry   be - to - Thee, O - Lord.

Then we would urge that church music should be chaste, severe, and simple in its style: that is to say, that all superadded embellishment, any phrase introduced for mere effect, should be rigidly excluded.

" In church music," says Hooker, " curiosity and ostentation of art, wanton, or light, or unsuitable harmony, such as only pleaseth the ear, and doth not naturally serve to the very kind and degree of those impressions which the matter that goeth with it leaveth in men's minds, doth rather blemish and disgrace that we do, than add beauty or furtherance unto it [7]."

[7] One thing that needs but to be mentioned to be condemned, is the taking airs from a secular composition, and applying them to sacred words. As we said before, it is almost impossible to avoid a similarity in some of the phrases of sacred and of secular music ; but to take an entire composition intended for a light love song, to adapt to it some of those words that are sung even in heaven, is not permissible to Handel himself. Let us take, for example, the well known song, " Dove sei," otherwise known

If we may now again return to our comparison of the prose and of the metrical versions of the Psalms, as regards their adaptation to divine worship, we shall find the superiority of the former over the latter, not less in the music to which they are sung, than in any other circumstance. To sing a metrical psalm-tune more than three or

as "Holy, holy, Lord God Almighty," and ask how it is possible, that music composed to suit the first set of words can with decency be adapted to the second.

" Dove sei,	amato	bene?	Vieni, l'alma	a
" *Holy*	*holy, Lord God Al-*	*mighty;*	*Holy,* *holy*	*who*
consolar,	a consolar.	Son	oppresso	da tormenti, &c.
was and is and is to come.	*For*	*Thou*	*only art holy, &c.*	

It may be urged in reply, that the themes of some of Handel's sublimest music in the Messiah are taken from his secular compositions; but such is the inherent sublimity of Handel's style, that much of his secular music is far better qualified for admission into the Church, than the professedly serious compositions of inferior masters.

Amongst dissenters, especially the lower grades of their most infinitesimal subdivisions, it is very common indeed to sing (so called) hymns to the most jovial tunes, such as the " King of the Cannibal Islands," or the " British Grenadier:" whilst such compositions as " Drink to me only," " Glorious Apollo," " Breathe soft, ye winds," and " Ah perdona," are sung in the more respectable meeting-houses, and it is to be doubted whether our churches are quite free from them. The famous Rowland Hill is said to have defended this practice, on the plea that the devil ought not to have all the fine music to himself; yet surely a more reverent spirit might have suggested that what was fit for the devil's service, was hardly fit for our Creator.

four times, even to the best tune, would be tiresome to a degree; in fact, it is never attempted: hence a Psalm, unless of that limited number of verses, can never be sung through; and this kind of music can never be used for the right office of music, which is to enhance the beauty of the Psalms as a whole.

But amongst the short compositions, or *chants*, as they are called, to which the prose version is sung, may be found some of the most perfect specimens of what church music ought to be. Those which are commonly called the Gregorian tones, and many of those also which were harmonized by Tallis and other church composers at the period of the Reformation, contain melodies which are almost coeval with Christianity itself, which formed the solace of those saints and martyrs to whom, under Providence, we owe the spread of the Gospel. They are severe, solemn, and reverential; nothing of earth seems to cleave to them. They breathe the chastened fervour of those who praise God, and yet, loaded with the consciousness of infirmity, know they cannot praise Him worthily; who love God, and yet feel they do not love Him as they ought; but yet look up to Him with affectionate reliance on his goodness and mercy. Why then abandon them, "sweeter," as they are, " than honey, and the honeycomb," for the doggrel metre and the miserable psalm-tune?

Although it must be confessed that some later

chants are far too florid, yet in almost every collection these bear a very small proportion to the others, and it may safely be said that none are so offensive to a proper taste as the modern hymn tunes.

It is only in fact when the Psalms are chanted in alternate verses by the opposite sides of the choir or congregation, that the divine spirit of poetry with which they are imbued, is at all set forth in a way to reach both the understanding and the heart. Let us willingly accord to any version or paraphrase all the merit it deserves; let the passages chosen for metrical psalmody be the very sublimest of the whole Psalm; let the tunes be chosen from grave old masters;—yet it must be evident that the meaning and purport of the Psalm, as a whole, must be lost. Take the 104th, for example; how can the scope of it, showing forth as it does the majesty of God, the wonders of creation, his bountiful care of all his creatures, their consequent dependence on Him, the joy of the just, and the destruction of the wicked, how can these be fairly expressed in the two or three verses which are usually selected for what people call the *singing Psalm*, in contra-distinction to the *reading Psalm?*

We would thus most earnestly contend for the restitution to the Psalms of the day, and to the responses, of such music as may be "both an ornament to God's service, and a help to our devotion:"

and we would most strenuously deprecate the neglect of music where it would come in regular order, and the substitution of inferior extraneous psalmody, which adds to the length of the service, and disturbs its just arrangement.

But yet, as there is a place provided for an anthem, both in the morning and afternoon service, and as anthems, metrical psalms, and hymns, are accustomed to be sung for the " comfort of such as delight in music," before or after the sermon, there certainly can be no objection to using a portion of any good paraphrase of the Psalms at these times, provided it be not done to the neglect of the chanting, and that the melody be one of those few old choral compositions, which are fit to be introduced into the service of the Church. Or, instead of these, hymns may be used, if care be taken that their language and sentiments, and the music they are accompanied with, are worthy of admission into the church. Unfortunately, however, there are many collections of modern hymns, which are as mean and commonplace in their diction, as they are irreverent and audacious in their sentiments; whilst as for the music they are sung to, it is impossible to find words degrading enough to express its most unredeemable meanness and vulgarity. It never rises above the level of the dullest mannerism; the same whining cadences; the same crawling minor to represent contrition, and the jig-like dotted quavers for praise. How frequently, too, a nonsensical repetition, is made of two or three words at the beginning of a line; as in the following example, taken from a hymn, which, shame to say, is sung in a church in the episcopal city of Winchester:

> " My poor pol-
> My poor pol-
> My poor pol-luted soul to save[8]."

If hymns are ever to be introduced into our service under due authority, it is to be hoped that they will rather be derived from the pure fountain of primitive Christianity, than be the original com-

---

[8] It would be both tedious and painful to make a catalogue of the carelessnesses and vulgarities observable in certain hymns that are permitted to be sung even in our churches—e. g. " With joy we *meditate the grace*," which is nonsense; " When *he the Baptist;*" and " When *he the tempting lawyer* came;" expressions which are any thing but English; " We *scarlet-coloured sinners*," which is a ludicrous perversion of a scriptural metaphor. Dissenters often make their hymns, as they do their extempore prayers, not so much praise to God, as controversial statements of some favourite tenet. Those modern Sadducees, the Socinians, have a hymn in defence of freethinking and the abuse of private judgment, which runs thus:—

> " Impostors hate the light,
> And dread each curious eye;
> Thy doctrines, Lord, our search invite," &c. &c.

positions of modern poets.   Without seeking to
disparage any efforts, however humble, to express
the praises of God in new and original poetry, yet
we cannot but feel that the old are better.   The
worship of the Infinite and Eternal is surely not
a thing to be varied by place, time, or circumstances.
They who hope to join the saints above, in " singing
the song of Moses the servant of God, and the
song of the Lamb," would rather cling to the
words which their forefathers in the faith sung
before them.   There are many hymns of the age
of the " Te Deum" and " Veni, Creator," the
only specimens which our Prayer-book contains of
the hymns of the primitive Church, which are well
worthy to be placed side by side with the Liturgy,
which for the most part is derived from the same
source [s].

Respecting anthems, as those compositions are
called which consist of passages of Scripture set to
music, we have only to say, that they are the glory
of the English Church, and that whenever they can
be sung well, they are most appropriately mingled
with the choral service, instead of metrical psalms
or hymns : but they ought not to be thought of,
until the integral parts of the service itself are
performed as they should be.

[s] Many ancient hymns have been translated by Bishop Mant,
Mr. Chandler, and others ; and that munificent benefactor of
the Church, A. J. B. Hope, Esq., has published a small collection in blank verse ; that is, in metre, but not in rhyme.

There is one part of divine service, in which, more than in any other, music would seem naturally pointed out by reason, and sanctioned by ancient usage, but in which it has now almost entirely fallen into disuse; we allude, of course, to the celebration of the Holy Communion. We know that our Saviour sung a hymn at its first institution; in the early church it was always customary, (the chanter singing with a divine melody, says one of the fathers, "O taste and see how gracious the Lord is,") and we have in our Liturgy, two of those hymns, which, as we are taught, have been sung in heaven. Certainly, if the most exalted benefits demand the deepest gratitude, it is difficult to conceive why the most appropriate form of expressing that gratitude should be neglected.

In the preceding pages we have endeavoured, at some length, to show the evident principles upon which—taking our service as we find it in the Prayer-book, and considering it as the public common act of intelligent beings,—an attempt may be made with success to give a spirit and reality where now there is only form. But it must be very evident to any one who considers the temper of the times, that to carry the attempt into execution must be a work of some time and trouble and difficulty. Not that such a consideration need deter any one who considers the vital importance of the subject.

The scheme which the writer would venture to propose is as follows :—

In every parish there are some persons who can sing,—in London parishes some members at least, in almost every family which attends the church.

Let then some persons in any given parish, whose hearts are in the cause, wait upon the clergy, and request their countenance and assistance, in forming a *Parochial Association for the Promotion of Church Music.* If the clergy make the first movement so much the better.

Such association should consist of as many persons as possible belonging to any respectable class in society.

Each member should provide himself with the necessary music, (which would cost very little,) but no subscription should be required. The wealthier members would, no doubt, make such donations as would defray the expenses of the association, and provide music for those who cannot afford to buy it.

The permission of the clergy and other authorities should then be requested that the members should meet, with the organist, and such of the children as can sing decently [8], to practise. The

[8] For a child to sing well enough for the service of the Church, it ought to be able to read very well, and to pronounce English correctly. It ought to be old enough also to understand the sense of what is sung, and to have received some

Sunday morning affords ample time—much of which is commonly wasted in bed;—every body is then at leisure, and they might sing for an hour before morning service,—in the church or school-room, according to circumstances.

As no man works well unless well paid, it is desirable that the organist should be properly remunerated for his extra trouble;—or else that some other properly qualified person or persons be engaged to superintend the singing at first.

There is such liberality evinced in the building and decorating of churches, and providing organs, that it is confidently hoped that a little more money would not be grudged in order that the service may be made worthy of the church and of the congregation.

At first, it would be desirable to take pains to sing better those things which are sung already, before attempting any thing new; but it may be confidently predicted that this would soon lead to an universal demand for more. Whilst the singing is done badly, people are careless about it;—let it be done well, and the desire for still further improvement would soon show itself.

Then pains should be taken to learn an harmonized Amen, so that this most important response may be given with the heart and voice of the whole congregation.

instruction in the Scriptures. Without these qualifications, the attempt to make children sing leads only to horrible discord.

Afterwards, the versicles and responses might be introduced by degrees, the melody being that of the ancient *plain chant*, very slightly harmonized. In the first instance, the versicles before the Psalms should be sung : and if that be done to Tallis's sublime harmonies, he must be dull indeed, who could bear to hear the Psalms prosaically read afterwards. Tallis's entire responses and Litany might be introduced afterwards, for festivals ; but the responses should always be unaccompanied by the organ[9].

In practising for the purpose of chanting the Psalms of the day, great care and pains are necessary. In the first place, the Psalm itself must be well understood ; and the clergyman would perhaps be willing to expound any obscure passages, such as many in the 68th Psalm, for instance. Then there must be no *gabbling :* the words must be clearly and distinctly enunciated in a solemn recitation, and all the stops be kept. The Gregorian and other old single chants are by far the best, the simplest, and the most devotional.

The Te Deum and other canonical hymns should be practised at first to single chants, and then to

[9] The author hopes to be able to publish the responses arranged in the simplest form for congregational use, and a collection of chants, for a few pence, so that there may be no difficulty on the score of expense. A specimen of the *plain chant* is given at page 21, and Tallis's versicles at page 19 ; and the writer has introduced them in order that people who rail vaguely against chanting the Liturgy may see what the character of the music really is.

some of the simpler compositions of Boyce, Tallis, &c. The practice of stringing together two or three verses of the Te Deum in chanting, spoils the effect of this noble hymn, and should always be avoided.

It is not contemplated that there should be a separate choir or orchestra of singers, the main body of the congregation being silent listeners; but that the singers should be dispersed over the whole church; every person in his own place audibly, but unostentatiously, joining in the service. For a congregation to turn their backs on the minister and stare up at the organ gallery, listening to a solo, executed by a female with all theatrical flourish and execution, is any thing but what becomes the service of the Church. It would be desirable, nevertheless, to have some boys who can sing well, and a few singers placed on opposite sides, near the clergyman, so as to lead the rest of the congregation.

A notice might be affixed to the church door, (as is the case at St. Paul's, Knightsbridge,) of the music intended to be performed during the week, so that such of the congregation, as have not leisure or opportunity for attending the public practising, might study their parts beforehand at home.

Any attempt at *fine* music, or solos, should be sedulously discouraged, till the grand object is attained of a full choral response and chant; and even then it should be done seldom and very discreetly.

We most firmly hope and believe, that if in any parish a few spirited individuals, under the guidance of the clergyman, were to put this plan in execution, and the service were found to be conducted with greater solemnity and impressiveness, the music being of a simple and easily-remembered kind; that many persons would join the association, that the example would spread, and that our churches then would present the cheering spectacle of a grand public solemnity, celebrated in spirit and in form as it ought to be.

As zeal on one side begets it on the other, so the clergyman would soon find the comfort and propriety of using the musical intonation, as a means of giving impressiveness to his part of the service, and of producing the feeling of hearty concurrence and unity between himself and his flock.

It were to be wished that some of the most influential of the clergy and laity would form a "Central Association" or *Society for the Promotion of Church Music*; whose object should be to publish and circulate tracts calculated to stir up the minds of the people; to publish good music at a very cheap rate; to provide teachers for poor parishes; and to be able to organize a select choir of gentlemen who, on the occasion of great religious festivals, or the consecration of churches, &c., might assemble, and celebrate a service really worthy of our Church and nation. How would the aisles of Westminster Abbey be thronged with worshippers, if instead of five-and-twenty, there were a hundred well-trained voices singing the sublime music of Purcell, or Greene, or Croft, or giving some reality to Blow's splendid effort to imitate the hallelujahs sung by multitudes in heaven; or if, instead of deserting the Lord's table, an augmented choir remained to give due grandeur to the sublimest of the Christian mysteries!

We will venture to say, that it would give immense gratification to every true lover of the Church to find the bishops and clergy mixing with the people and encouraging them in an earnest endeavour to render the public service what it ought to be, in all outward respects. If the parish clergy were to take the music under their own superintendence, even although under the present maimed and miserable system, yet what a horde of carelessnesses and irregularities might be prevented. How common it is to hear part of the children singing one verse of a Psalm, and another part a different one; or the organist playing to the first Psalm the tune meant for the second; or three or four verses of some Psalm sung, the last of which ends merely in a comma, the sense being incom-

plete; (as in the first three verses of the eighth
Psalm, which the writer has repeatedly heard sung
by themselves;) all which things are enough to
make any earnest man blush for his religion[1].

The organ, too, what benefits might be derived
from a little wholesome looking after both what is
played and the style of the performance. As
things stand, we have no hesitation in saying that
the organ has contributed as much as anything to
the decay of congregational singing; for in the
first place, after the organ has been set up, and an
organist appointed with a salary, the parish authorities imagine that all has been done that there is
any need for, and never think of engaging a choir
to sing either for love or money; and in the next
place, fifteen or twenty stops of the full organ
render it a matter of perfect indifference as to how
people sing, or whether, in fact, they sing at all.
Often and often has the writer been in a church
where, with an overpowering organ, not three people in the whole church opened their mouths.
But the surest method of all, to extinguish anything

[1] Another very common way of turning God's praise into
ridicule, is the singing the hymn, " Awake, my soul, and with
the sun," somewhere about noon. This hymn, an imitation of
the ancient " Jam lucis orto sidere," is evidently intended for
sunrise; but yet a lazy London congregation, unmindful that
the sun has run half his daily race, may be heard to sing it at
their morning prayer, beginning at half-past eleven.

like singing, is to set up a grinding organ". Truly, if a foreigner entered some of our churches he might imagine that, as a great manufacturing community, we employed machinery in the service of God, as well as in other things.

How often, too, between the verses of some mawkish psalm-tune, is the time of the congregation occupied by a long theatrical symphony,—symphony indeed it would be wrong to call it, for it has no connexion with the tune, and is merely intended to exhibit the manual dexterity of the operator; but worse than any other abomination is that often exhibited in the voluntary before the

² They who really love our old English virtues and customs, must have frequent occasion to lament the gradual progress of degeneracy, in the substitution of these odious machines for the ancient village choir with their simple instruments. Badly enough, perhaps, they sing; time and tune may suffer rude encounters; and shocking may the old blacksmith's bassoon sound in the ears of the squire's daughters, on their return from a London visit, filled with fine ideas of " pictures, taste, Shakspeare, and the musical glasses." But surely these men are made of the right stuff; their hearts are in the work; their occupation gave them a tie to the church which it were unwise to sever; and with patience, and encouragement, and instruction, they might be made the nucleus of a true congregational choir. The writer once heard a clergyman say, that for years his parish choir sang *Nunc Dimittis* after the second lesson, without his knowing what it was, and he always read it too. All right thinkers will say, More shame for him.

first lesson. After meanly reading and muttering the Psalms, down sit the congregation with a self-satisfied air to listen to the performance of a piece of music. If it be a devotional composition, it seems the height of absurdity to offer to the Deity the music of an organ, and refuse that of our own voices; but often enough it consists of some operatic air—*Dove sono*, from Rossini's Nozze di Figaro, or *Ah perdona*, or some piece of the kind, overflowing with amatory tenderness, and embellished with all the brilliancy and skill which the player can put forth; then comes the first lesson, and flatly enough it falls upon the ear.

We must not be supposed, however, to throw the blame of this on the organist only, but rather on the modern system. Religious music of any kind is very little cultivated, and *church* music almost entirely unknown to the mass of the people. We might say that a very large body of the clergy seem quite unconscious that there is a greater propriety in one style of music for church purposes than in another; although *church* music, *par excellence*, differs as widely from the common dissenters' hymn-tunes as the cheerful and elevated piety of heart, soul, and intellect of which it is the echo, differs from gloomy, narrow-minded fanaticism.

If the clergy, in their natural capacity of educators of the people, were to cause the young persons —rich and poor—in the numerous institutions under their care, to be instructed in church music, expressly to enable them to join audibly in the church service, what a happy revolution might be accomplished. What possible harm could result if school-girls spared for this purpose some little of that time which they now devote so assiduously to master the fingering of some horribly discordant piano-forte piece, or to strain their feeble voices in singing Grisi's last new song — accomplishments which, as is well known, are abandoned by eight-tenths of them in a very few years, without, we fear, leaving behind them much to benefit the head or the heart. Would they be worse wives and mothers? Boys, too, might it not render them less prone to amusements of a low and sensual order? And with respect to the poorer orders, who that sees them daily, as the writer does, in their sordid habitations, can wonder that the husband should prefer spending part of his earnings at a public-house, instead of coming home to his ignorant slatternly wife, and forbear from wishing that they were made capable of joining with their children in chanting the Psalms, (the only way in which they can be sung worthily,) a recreation so full of cheerfulness and piety, able to give some charm to the humblest home, and some solace to the hardest lot—with the certainty that they would be enticed to pay more regular visits to the house of prayer, where, from the fountain of celestial wisdom, they might learn that godliness which is as profitable in this world, as it is full of hope for the world to come ?

Would it not be as well if the idea of *Holy* days were revived, so that the common people, instead of looking on the great festivals as times for vulgar merriment and debauchery, might be induced instead to flock to our cathedrals, and join in a magnificent choral worship ? Might not they thus acquire ideas of the sanctity of the place, that would be far better preservatives from the barbarous propensity to mutilate works of art, than the unhallowed scheme of spending the Lord's day in a picture gallery ?

But we can readily imagine some person saying, Why all this desire for innovation ? why not leave things alone ? does not everything go on well enough ? I have been at church all my life without finding anything amiss ; and so did my father before me : and I hate change ; it unsettles one's mind.

But we would ask in reply, Does everything go on as well as it ought ? is the condition of the masses, as they are called, what the politician and the moralist, or the religious man would desire ? Do we hear no complaints about the vice, ignorance, and ingratitude of the lower orders ; of their miserable poverty, increased tenfold (in great towns) by their own recklessness and improvidence ? And ought not the church services to be adapted rather to compel those loiterers about the highways and hedges to come in, than to suit you, whose education, and circumstances, and social position render you less prone to temptation, and less in need of instruction? Is it the whole or the sick that need a physician? the rich or the poor for whom the feast should be made?

In thus pleading as warmly as we can for the greater cultivation of Church Music, let it not be supposed that we do so as a mere matter of form, or taste, or ancient usage; on the contrary, we are convinced that it might be an instrument of the greatest moral and political benefit.

Looking on the Church in her lowest aspect, as an institution sanctioned by mere human authority, it cannot be denied that her political interests are threatened with danger. No one who regards the *spirit of the age* can believe that she will long retain, undivided, the privileges of being *the* Church established by law. What Parliament can give, it can also take away; and history teaches us that they who ought to have been her champions, have been her plunderers and oppressors; and what has been, may yet be again. Moreover, her peril is not only from without; for alas! it is impossible to conceive of any religious community, in which, with so much sterling piety and fervent zeal amongst some, there is yet such a profound ignorance of her origin, nature, and antiquity, of the nature and intent of her rites and ceremonies, of her peculiar privileges as a member of Christ's body, and of her claims to the allegiance of her children, as there is amongst a great mass of so-called members of the Church of England. As for that feeling of *esprit de corps*, of brotherhood or mutual attachment amongst us, because members of the same household of faith, where is it to be found? Gigantic as the sums of money are, which are annually subscribed for church purposes, yet they are as dust in the balance, compared with the contributions of sectarians in proportion to their numbers. The very outcasts too of any tribe of schismatics are reckoned amongst her members, and can get into parish vestries, and coerce the clergyman and beard the bishop, and under pretence of a holy zeal for " our pious Reformers," and the purity of religion, may interfere with the services of the sanctuary, and spread alarm and dissension amongst the people.

How deficient too is our ordinary service of any thing that can appeal to the imagination of the young. Children, as Mr. Gresley admirably observes, may be taught the Catechism and Thirty-nine Articles, and be able to prove them by Scripture at a public examination ; they may be taught, in the abstract, the great truths of religion, and their duty to God and their neighbour; but yet these things go no further than the head ; they do not reach the heart; and when children go to church, where what they learn theoretically ought to be realized, there the service is a cold form, lacking, as far as the congregation are concerned, earnestness, reverence, and spirituality.

Consider, too, the festivals of the Church; are they celebrated in a way to impress the young, that we really believe what we profess? They, whose souls are so readily touched by emotion, and in whom God Himself has planted the irresistible impulse to express their emotion by every outward sound and gesture, are taught that some solemn seasons are set apart for repentance and sorrow for sin, and that others are devoted to joy and thanksgiving, for the commemoration of various events connected with the most transcendant benefits to every human being personally. But how is this difference expressed? There is the same cold gloom about our parish churches, the same dismal psalmody; and the only thing to mark the high festival, which ought to engross the feelings of every one, is, that the clergyman calls out " the collect for Whitsunday" before saying the peculiar prayer for the day.

In fact, in our ordinary service, there is nothing for the young to *love*. But the Church might surely imitate what we see of God's own doings in the world around us. He has not dressed the world in Quaker hue; and we find no visible sign in creation that the mean and vulgar are pleasing in his sight, or of the dissenting maxim, that a contempt of outward form and beauty can be a type of in-dwelling spirituality and holiness. And if God, for his own glory and our delight, has decked the flowers of the field with every splendour of colour, and filled the air with the melody of birds, and if the mere sight of the cheerful earth, crowned with beauty and goodness, can infuse serenity into the soul, surely we may take of these his gifts, and offer them to Him, and not think harmonious form or sound or colour misplaced in his house, or that they may not lawfully be used to attract those affections He has given us, into the highest and purest channel.

Like the statesman, who said he cared not who made the people's laws, so that he made their ballads, we would say, Teach your children the music of the church, and you will have their affections at least enlisted on your side. But, as matters are conducted at present, it is not wonderful that the young, when emancipated from school, should have no great affection for a church which does so little to attract them, or that in soberer years they should fall so readily into the snares of dissent.

It is quite erroneous to suppose that dissent is caused only by a want of clergymen of the Church, or by their carelessness in doing their duty. On the contrary, the writer has been told by evangelical clergymen, that it notoriously abounds most where the doctrines of the Gospel are fully preached, and where the minister is zealous. An old and truly pious clergyman, against whose doctrines no evangelical dissenter could say a word, lamented most feelingly to the writer the perpetual defalcation of his parishioners; such of them as seemed to have received serious religious impressions being watched and proselytized by the ever-busy emissaries of schism.

But surely it is not very difficult to give something like a rational reason—in part at least—for this unhappy facility. What means have these poor people had of ever acquiring anything like *Church feeling?* If they go into a church, and into a dissenting meeting-house, and in both hear the same hymn to the same drawling tune at the beginning of the service, and another of the same character before or after the sermon,—what is there to impress their mind palpably with any difference of *system*, or to prevent their believing that the only difference is, that the *dissenting minister* preaches and prays out of his own head, whilst the *church gentleman*, with the help of a clerk, reads his prayers and sermons out of a book;—the white-washed walls and high pews being the same perhaps in both cases?

Looking then to Church Music, whether as a mere political means of producing uniformity of sentiment, or as one vehicle of divine truth to the soul, and a means of infixing it there, we would urge its claims on the attention of our spiritual superiors. We would earnestly hope that the clergy might be induced to study it, as a most necessary preparation for their sacred calling. We should love to see them mingling with their flock —rich and poor together—animating them in their attempts to add every decent grandeur to their common prayer; breaking down the painful barrier of restraint and unfamiliarity which now exists to such a degree that the clergyman is a personal stranger to more than half his parish; and directing them practically in their devotions in this world, instead, as is the common case, of being called in only when they are on the point of leaving it. How admirable it would be to have provision made in every school, from Winchester and Eton, down to the union workhouse school, that the rising generation should be taught what is such a safeguard in youth, such a solace in age and affliction, such a pleasure always and everywhere. Then might the Church be united at home and extending abroad; her temples resounding with—

" Creed of the saint, and anthem of the blest,"

and " *O quam dilecta,*" the constant song of her children.

*** THE following works will be useful to any one who wishes to cultivate Church Music:—

THE CHORAL SERVICE OF THE UNITED CHURCH OF ENGLAND AND IRELAND, by the Rev. JOHN JEBB, M. A., 8vo. *Parker.*

THE BOOK OF COMMON PRAYER, WITH MUSICAL NOTES; with an Appendix, containing a Dissertation on Plain Tune and the Gregorian Chant; edited by W. DYCE, Esq., M. A., *Burns.*

THE PSALTER, POINTED FOR CHANTING; by R. JANES: with the Gregorian Tones. *Burns.*

HYMNS OF THE CHURCH, WITH TALLIS'S RESPONSES, &c., by SAMUEL PEARSALL. *Burns.*

GREGORIAN AND OTHER ECCLESIASTICAL CHANTS, WITH TALLIS'S VERSICLES, &c. *Burns.* Price 2s. 6d.—This is the very best collection of Chants extant; simple, grave, and devotional.

TALLIS'S DAILY SERVICE; by BISHOP. *Cocks.*—This is an excellent edition. The preface shows the very great antiquity of much of the music of the English Church, which was harmonized and arranged, but not composed, by Tallis.

THE END.

GILBERT & RIVINGTON, Printers, St. John's Square, London.